Copyright © 2015 by Beautiful Books for Children
All rights reserved. This book or any portion thereof
may not be reproduced or used in any manner whatsoever
without the express written permission of the publisher
except for the use pictures of the interior in a book review.

Printed in the United States of America

First Printing, 2015

ISBN 0692507159

Beautiful Books for Children
1625 Walker Ave NW,
#141031,
Grand Rapids, MI 49514

www.BeautifulBooksforChildren.com

## About the Illustrator

Carolyn Yonkers is a children's book illustrator, and artist. You can find out more about her work on her website www.ArtByCT.com.

## About Beautiful Books for Children

Our mission is to support literacy, early childhood development, and positive bonds between children and those who care for them through books, coloring books, and parent resources. You can learn more at www.BeautifulBooksforChildren.com

www.ingramcontent.com/pod-product-compliance
Lightning Source LLC
Chambersburg PA
CBHW081501040426
42446CB00016B/3351